Lost Railways of Dundalk and the N

including railways of Cos. Louth, Meath, West N Monaghan, Navan, Cavan and Longford
by Stephen Johnson

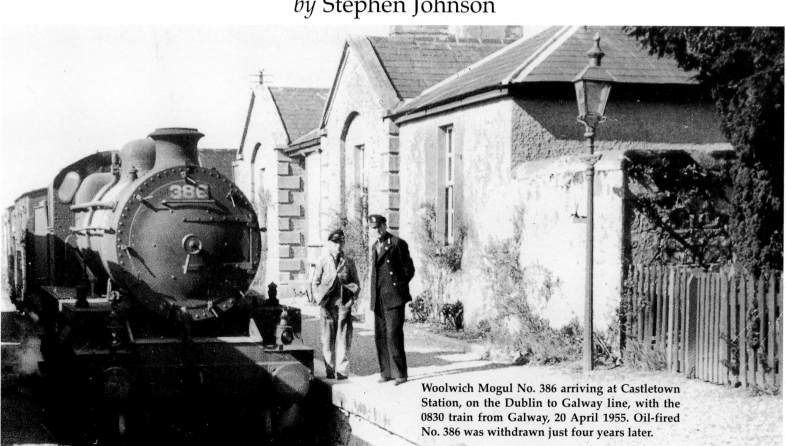

Woolwich Mogul No. 386 arriving at Castletown Station, on the Dublin to Galway line, with the 0830 train from Galway, 20 April 1955. Oil-fired No. 386 was withdrawn just four years later.

Text © Stephen Johnson, 2006.
First Published in the United Kingdom, 2006
Stenlake Publishing Limited
54–58 Mill Square
Catrine
KA5 6RD
www.stenlake.co.uk
ISBN 9781840333701

The terminus station at Oldcastle.

The publishers regret that they cannot supply copies of any pictures featured in this book.

The publishers wish to thank the following for contributing photographs to this book: John Alsop for the front cover, pages 47 and 48, and the inside back cover; Richard Casserley for the inside front cover, pages, 1, 4—15, 18—26, 28, 30, 32, 35—44, 46, and the back cover.

INTRODUCTION

Dundalk, in County Louth, was a major railway centre for over a century, being appended the sobriquet the 'Railway Town'. It was here that the Great Northern Railway of Ireland had its main workshops next to the main line railway from Dublin to Belfast. An interesting feature for many years was the 'square crossing', just south of the station. It was here that the Irish North Western Railway crossed the Dublin–Belfast line at right–angles and on the level, much to the consternation of the railway inspectors. The scene of many a collision and other knocks, the crossing was removed in 1954.

From Dundalk, the Irish North Western Railway snaked its way across Ireland via Clones, Enniskillen and Omagh to serve the city of Londonderry. To the east, the London & North Western Railway owned Dundalk, Newry & Greenore Railway made its way along the coast to the port of Greenore, remaining British-owned until closure. Clones was once a major railway junction, with the Dundalk–Londonderry line crossing the Belfast–Cavan line. Sadly, this once busy junction has not seen any trains since 1960.

The county town of Navan in County Meath sat at the crossroads of the Great Northern Railway of Ireland (GNR(I)) line from Drogheda to Oldcastle and the Midland Great Western Railway (MGWR) line from Clonsilla to Kingscourt, once proposed as a possible inland route from Dublin to Belfast. Although passenger services have long ceased, the remaining parts of this line were kept busy with gypsum, zinc ore and cement traffic.

Numerous branch lines diverged off the major routes to serve other centres of traffic. The Cootehill branch was once intended to reach Cavan but ended at Cootehill when a rival scheme to Cavan was announced. The Belturbet branch ran off the Cavan line at Ballyhaise and met up with the Cavan & Leitrim narrow gauge railway, producing an interesting mixed gauge operation with coal traffic being manually transferred right up until closure. At Cavan, the GNR(I) met the MGWR with an end-on junction. The station was unusual in having a passenger footbridge at platform level that divided the platform in two, with GNR(I) trains using the northern end and the MGWR using the southern end. There was, of course, a connecting line for transfers.

The decline of the railways began in earnest after the First World War with political changes and increased competition from road transport. In 1921, the Irish Free State was established in the south with Dublin as its capital. Partition followed and the GNR(I) found itself operating in two political states, crossing the newly created border no less than seventeen times. Cross-border customs inspections were carried out at various customs posts such as Dundalk, Clones and Glaslough. This necessarily delayed traffic and journey times were increased. In the meantime, the railways of the Free State were amalgamated in 1924 to form the Great Southern Railway.

With traffic flows disrupted and revenue falling, the railways had to make economies. Amongst these was the introduction of railbuses on the GNR(I) system and the Dundalk, Newry & Greenore Railway in the 1930s. These railbuses could stop anywhere and many additional stops appeared in the timetable, mainly at level crossings, in an effort to reach more passengers. The Second World War saw a vast increase in traffic and the financial worries receded for the time being. However, the post-war period saw the problems return with a vengeance.

The GNR(I)'s finances became critical in 1950 when the company ran out of money. By the end of the year, the shareholders agreed that the company should close the line. Faced with the end of rail transport in a large part of Ireland, the two governments entered into talks with the company. In the early 1951, the company announced that it would end services in Northern Ireland and gave notice to some 1,200 staff. This was withdrawn when the two governments agreed to meet the shortfall and support the company's operation. In 1953, the two governments jointly purchased and operated the company, and the GNR(I) was renamed the Great Northern Railway Board to reflect the change in status. This proved to be a temporary reprieve when differences in opinion on the future of rail transport culminated with the Northern Minister of Commerce announcing proposals to close some 115 miles of railway in 1956, including the Portadown—Tynan line and Newtownbutler—Omagh section of the Dundalk—Londonderry line. This would have a devastating effect on the remaining parts of the line, with the only access being via Dundalk. Despite various tribunals and public hearings, the Northern minister eventually had his way and announced that all services would cease at the end of

September 1957. The GNRB was left with a difficult situation and decided that it was not worthwhile to try and continue to operate services on what was left. An application to close the remaining parts of the affected lines and branches was made, but although agreement was given, it was not possible to get the legislation through by the end of the month. As a result, with the closure of parts of the system on 1 October 1957, the GNRB were left to operate the 'stump' lines, as they were called, for a further two weeks until they too were closed on 14 October 1957.

Meanwhile, in June 1957 the Northern Minister of Commerce announced his intention to end the agreement to jointly operate the GNRB. As a result, legislation was passed through both parliaments and the GNRB ceased to exist from 1 October 1958. The remaining lines and assets were passed to the Ulster Transport Authority and Córas Iompair Éireann. Although passenger services had ceased, CIÉ now inherited the remaining freight operation and it was not long before those lines were closed, all having gone by 1960.

Since the 1960s, Dublin has grown with the surrounding areas becoming dormitory towns. Existing lines have seen an increase in commuter services and there are now plans to reopen the line from Clonsilla to Dunboyne and maybe as far as Navan.

In this book, we start our journey through the North East by looking at the two MGWR lines in the area, Clonsilla to Kingscourt and the Athboy branch. Moving on to the GNR(I), the Drogheda to Oldcastle line is next, followed by the Ardee branch off the Dublin to Belfast main line. Then, moving north to the 'Railway Town', we look at the British-owned Dundalk, Newry & Greenore line before moving on to the Irish North. The various branches off the Irish North are covered as well as the former Ulster Railway route to Clones from Portadown. Cavan features next with the GNR(I) line from Clones and the Belturbet branch before looking at the MGWR line to Cavan and its branch to Killeshandra. In conclusion, there is a list of closed stations on lines still operating.

Cavan, 18 April 1955. This station was unusual in that the northern end was served by the GNR(I) while the southern end was served by CIÉ.

Clonsilla to Kingscourt

Passenger service withdrawn	27 January 1947	*Stations closed*	*Date*
Distance	43½ miles	Navan	27 January 1947
Company	Midland Great Western Railway	Proudstown Park	27 January 1947
		Gibbstown	27 January 1947
Stations closed	*Date*	Wilkinstown	27 January 1947
Clonsilla *	Open	Castletown Halt	1935
Dunboyne	27 January 1947	Nobber	27 January 1947
Fairyhouse Bridge **	1931	Kilmainham Wood	27 January 1947
Batterstown	27 January 1947	Kingscourt	27 January 1947
Drumree	27 January 1947		
Kilmessan Junction	27 January 1947		
Bective	27 January 1947	* Closed 10 November 1947; reopened 30 November 1981.
Navan (Temporary Terminus)	1869	** Race traffic only from 1931 to c.1940.

Ex-GNR(I) Qs class 4-4-0 No. 132N, arriving at Dunboyne with a special for Kingscourt, 3 June 1961.

Batterstown Station, facing Kingscourt, 3 June 1961.

The county of Meath, just to the north west of County Dublin, has two important towns that were early targets for rail connection, Navan and Kells. The first successful line to reach Navan was opened in 1850 by the Dublin & Drogheda Railway. The D&D also planned an extension to Kells and the government, mindful of the indirect route of the line from Dublin to Kells via Drogheda, stipulated that if another more direct railway was built to Navan, that company would have automatic running powers over the D&D to Kells.

Drumree Station, facing Kingscourt, 3 June 1961.

A few years later, a proposal for a more direct line from Dublin to Navan was made. This new line would leave the Midland & Great Western Railway (MGWR) at Clonsilla and run north to Navan with a branch serving Athboy and Trim. After considerable negotiation, an Act was finally obtained by the Dublin & Meath Railway in 1858. The first sod was turned by the Duke of Leinster on 21 October 1858 and construction carried on until the line was ready for inspection in 1862. In the meantime, the Dublin & Meath Railway entered negotiations with the MGWR to work the line. There was disagreement over the financial arrangements and for running over the MGWR from Clonsilla to Dublin. This led to the D&M applying for powers to build its own line into Dublin with a terminus in Eccles Street. The matter was taken to arbitration and a settlement reached, with the MGWR working the line and running from Clonsilla to the MGWR's Broadstone terminus.

Kilmessan Junction Station, 3 June 1961. This was the junction for the Athboy branch, which can be seen diverging to the left.

The line was nearing completion in 1862 and the D&M directors informed the D&D that they wanted to use the running powers stipulated in the D&D's 1847 Act to run to Kells. Needless to say, disagreement followed and the matter was referred to arbitration. Meanwhile the line was finally completed and, after an inspection, was opened for traffic on 29 August to a separate station in Navan just to the south of the D&D's station. The dispute over running to Kells was finally resolved and the D&M announced that through trains would run to Kells from 1 December. A quarter-mile connecting line had been built from the D&M station to connect with the D&D line, but the signalling arrangements were not ready by the commencement date. The service was postponed until proper arrangements had been made, which in the event, was just two weeks later on 15 December. Oddly enough, the connecting spur line had been refused approval by the Board of Trade and does not appear to have ever been approved! A fare war followed as both companies competed for traffic. An amicable agreement was reached in the summer of 1863 and both companies settled down for the time being. A new station at Batterstown, between Dunboyne and Kilmessan, was opened in July 1863.

Bective Station, 3 June 1961.

The extension to Kingscourt was proposed in 1864 and a separate company, the Navan & Kingscourt Railway, received an Act in 1865. No sooner had this been done that more proposals were being made to extend the line further from Kinsgcourt to Castleblayney to connect with the Irish North Western Railway. In the meantime, no work had been carried out on the original proposal and the N&K had to go back to Parliament to seek an extension of time in 1867. Although working agreements with the D&M had been arranged, another extension of time was sought in 1870 and construction finally started.

Gibbstown Station, 3 June 1961.

A year earlier matters had come to a head between the D&M and the MGWR over working arrangements, something that had been a constant source of difficulty. The MGWR eventually forced the D&M to accept its working arrangements in June 1869. The consequences of the arrangement were that the Kells trains ceased to run from September, but to maintain the connection, a new station would be built at the junction of the D&M and D&D. Navan Junction station opened in 1869 and consequently the old D&M station was closed.

Further north, the first part of the Kingscourt line had been completed and was ready for opening. The section between Navan and Kilmainham Wood was finally opened, after three inspections, on 1 November 1872. The extension left the line a quarter of a mile from Navan Junction Station at Kingscourt Junction. Kingscourt Junction has also been known as Nevinstown Junction and Navan West Junction. The N&K however were in financial difficulty and could not complete the remaining part of the line to Kingscourt. Their position ended up with the company in Chancery in 1873 whereupon their capital was rearranged. This move enabled the contractor to complete the work by 1875. The Board of Trade inspected the line and requested that further work be carried out. The contractor refused as he was owed money, resulting in a take-over by the company's chairman who carried out the necessary work. With this done, the Kilmainham Wood to Kingscourt section opened on 1 November 1875. Meanwhile, the short section between Navan Junction and Kingscourt Junction had been doubled.

Although an initial approach to the D&M in 1880 was unsuccessful, the MGWR did eventually purchase the D&M and the N&K in 1889. The racecourse at Fairyhouse Bridge received a station around 1881, for race traffic only. Few changes were made to the Meath line under the MGWR and this continued under the GSR. An alteration to the junction layout at Navan was made in 1911. Kingscourt Junction was taken out of use and the double-track line became two single parallel lines with the Kingscourt line diverging at this point. Between 1927 and 1931, Fairyhouse Bridge had a regular advertised passenger service. After 1931, it was still used for race specials until about 1940.

Kilmainham Wood Station, facing Kingscourt, 3 June 1961.

Fuel shortages during the Second World War caused the suspension of passenger services on 8 October 1941. Services were resumed in mid-1943, only to be withdrawn again the following year. 1945 saw the reinstatement of passenger services, but the hard winter and miners' strike of 1947 saw services suspended from 27 January with the goods service following in March. In the event, passenger services were not resumed.

Kingscourt Station, the end of the line, 3 June 1961.

Goods services continued until 1 April 1963 when CIÉ closed the Clonsilla to Navan Junction section. Gypsum had become a major source of traffic from Kingscourt and this traffic was now routed via Drogheda. Kingscourt Junction was reinstated in 1977 but is now called Tara Mines Junction. With the building of new residential areas to the north west of Dublin, the government is giving serious consideration to reopening the Clonsilla—Dunboyne section and possibly all the way to Navan.

Kilmessan Junction to Athboy

Passenger service withdrawn	27 January 1947
Distance	$12\frac{1}{4}$ miles
Company	Midland Great Western Railway

Stations closed	*Date*
Kilmessan Junction	27 January 1947
Trim	27 January 1947
Athboy	27 January 1947

Kilmessan Junction Station, facing Dublin, 3 June 1961.

The Athboy branch was built by the Dublin & Meath Railway and opened for traffic in stages. Kilmessan to Trim opened for goods on 15 December 1863 and to Athboy on 21 January 1864. Passenger services throughout commenced the following month on 26 February 1864. The line was worked by the Midland Great Western Railway. The branch was absorbed into the MGWR in 1889 along with the parent Meath company.

An ex-MGWR Kitson 0-6-0T replenishing its tanks at Athboy, 27 June 1939.

The wartime fuel shortage had an effect on the line early on with passenger services being suspended from 8 October 1941. The service was resumed after the war on 10 December 1945. However, this resumption of services was short lived and the passenger services were again suspended from 27 January 1947 due to the hard winter and miners' strike in Britain. Regular goods services were also suspended from 10 March 1947. In the event, this proved to be the end of the line for the branch as it never reopened. A weekly livestock train continued to run until 1953 and the line was officially closed on 15 March 1954. It lingered on for a few more years, being used for wagon storage before it was finally lifted from August 1958.

Drogheda to Oldcastle

Passenger service withdrawn	14 April 1958	*Stations closed*	*Date*
Distance	39¾ miles	Navan (old station)	1864
Company	Great Northern Railway of Ireland	Navan	27 January 1947
		Navan Junction *	14 April 1958
		Ballybeg	14 April 1958
Stations closed	*Date*	Kells	14 April 1958
Drogheda	Open	Virginia Road	14 April 1958
Duleek	14 April 1958	Oldcastle	14 April 1958
Lougher Halt	14 April 1958		
Beauparc	14 April 1958	* GNR(I) trains were not advertised to stop here between c.1941 to 1946.	

The shed at Drogheda Station, 5 September 1947. To the left is GNR(I) 0-6-0 SG2 No. 15, built by Nasmyth, Wilson in 1926. To the right, in the shed, is GNR(I) 0-6-0 NGQs No. 39, also built by Nasmyth, Wilson in 1911.

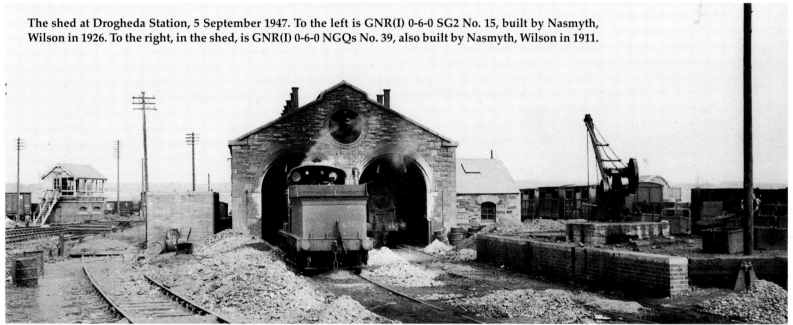

The history of the railways connecting Navan to the main railway system have been partially told in the first section of this book. The other line in the history is the Drogheda to Oldcastle line. The Dublin & Belfast Junction Railway received authority to build a line from Drogheda to Navan in 1845. However, as the line was to connect with the already completed Dublin & Drogheda Railway, a clause in an Act of 1847 stipulated that ownership of the line would be transferred to the D&D upon completion. As already recounted, another stipulation of the Act was that if another more direct railway was built between Dublin and Navan that company would have running rights over the line to Kells.

Navan GNR(I) station, facing Dublin, 3 June 1961.

The line was completed in 1850 and the line opened for traffic on 15 February. An intermediate station was provided at Beauparc with a second, Duleek, opening in the September. The extension to Kells continued from the Navan terminus westwards over the Navan Viaduct to Kells. The line opened for traffic on 11 July 1853. The rival Dublin & Meath Railway arrived at Navan in 1862 and had already announced their intention to use the running powers to Kells. A short connecting line was built from the D&M station to a junction three-quarters of a mile west of the D&D station at Navan Junction. 1856 saw Ballybeg, between Navan and Kells, receive a station.

Navan Junction Station, May 1948. The GNR(I) side was to the left and the CIÉ side to the right. A GNR(I) railbus can be seen at the platform with an Oldcastle service.

Although there was no real incentive to extend beyond Kells, another company had proposed extending to Cavan or Castleblayney. This threat resulted in the D&D extending through the sparsely inhabited countryside to Oldcastle. The extension was completed and opened for traffic on St Patrick's Day, 1863. One intermediate station at Virginia Road was provided, over six miles from the village it served. In 1864, the D&D opened a new station at Navan to the west of the viaduct. The old station was subsequently closed. Relations between the D&M and their working company, the MGWR, had deteriorated with the MGWR imposing new working conditions in 1869. The result of this saw the D&M trains to Kells stopping in September. However, to maintain a connection, a new station was built on the eastern side of the junction, known as Navan Junction Station. The Navan & Kingscourt Railway opened the first section of their line from to Navan Junction to Kilmainham Wood in 1872. The new line left the Oldcastle line a quarter of a mile from Navan Junction Station at Kingscourt Junction. Kingscourt Junction has also been known as Nevinstown Junction and Navan West Junction. With the opening of the final section to Kingscourt, this short section of line was doubled in 1875.

Kells Station, facing Oldcastle, 3 June 1961.

The D&D became part of the short-lived Northern Railway in 1875, which subsequently became part of the Great Northern Railway of Ireland in 1876. An alteration to the junction layout at Navan was made in 1911. Kingscourt Junction was taken out of use and the double-track line became two single parallel lines with the Kingscourt line diverging at this point. With the formation of the Irish Free State in 1921, partition ensued. In 1924 the government of the Free State decided to amalgamate all the line railways running wholly within the Free State into the Great Southern Railway. Companies operating services in both states were to remain independent and although the Drogheda—Oldcastle line was within the Free State it was operated by the GNR(I), which remained an independent company. The ever innovative GNR(I) introduced a railcar service on the line in 1940. The flexibility of railcar operation enabled the GNR(I) to stop virtually anywhere passengers might be had. The result of this flexibility saw a halt provided at Lougher, between Duleek and Beauparc. Other railcar stopping places were provided at various level crossings along the line, with some five crossings being designated in all.

The terminus station at Oldcastle, 3 June 1961.

Post-war traffic on all Irish railways fell and many found themselves in difficulty. The GNR(I) was badly affected, running out of money by 1950. As a result, the GNR(I) announced in January 1951 that it was to cease all services in Ulster. Goaded into action, the two governments of Ireland made a joint offer to purchase the company and the GNR(I) became the Great Northern Railway Board in 1953. This action only delayed the inevitable and railcar services from Navan to Oldcastle ceased in 1956. The Stormont government removed its support of the GNRB in 1957 and major closures soon ensued. Passenger services from Drogheda to Oldcastle were withdrawn on 14 April 1958. On 1 October 1958, the GNRB ceased to exist, with all lines in the Republic passing to CIÉ. The Navan to Oldcastle section was closed completely by CIÉ on 30 March 1961 and, with the closure of the former D&M route from Clonsilla to Navan on 1 April 1963, the gypsum traffic from Kingscourt was routed via Drogheda. In 1972 a new cement factory was opened two and three-quarter miles from Drogheda. The Platin Cement factory is rail connected and has a large number of sidings generating rail traffic. A further boost to the line came in 1977 when a half-mile section of line from Navan West Junction (Kingscourt Junction) to Oldcastle was reopened to serve Tara Mines. The junction was reinstated and is now called Tara Mines junction.

Dromin Junction to Ardee

Passenger service withdrawn	3 June 1934
Distance	5 miles
Company	Great Northern Railway of Ireland

Stations closed	*Date*
Dromin Junction	31 January 1955
Ardee	3 June 1934

Dromin Junction, 5 June 1964. A special train stands at the Ardee branch platform.

Ardee Station, 5 June 1964. It was built in the familiar yellow brick favoured by the GNR(I).

The town of Ardee was missed by less than five miles when the Dublin & Belfast Junction Railway opened their line in 1849. It was some years later when a scheme was proposed in 1884 to connect Ardee with the main line. This took the form of a roadside steam tramway and needless to say, the Great Northern Railway of Ireland, by this time the owners of the main line, opposed it. Instead, the GNR(I) put forward their own proposal for a short branch from a junction at Dromin a few years later in 1891. The proposal received an Act in June 1892 and construction had finished in 1896. Having passed an inspection, the five-mile branch opened for traffic on 1 August 1896. Although situated in the Free State, the branch remained part of the independent GNR(I) during the amalgamations of 1924.

The interior of Ardee Station, 5 June 1964 - almost exactly thirty years after it lost its passenger services.

The branch survived the 1933 strike only to lose its passenger service the following year on 3 June. The GNR(I) financial crisis in 1951 saw the branch come under the control of the newly formed Great Northern Railway Board from 1953. In 1958, the GNRB was dissolved with the branch passing to CIÉ. CIÉ continued to operate a goods service to Ardee until final closure came on 3 November 1975.

Dundalk to Greenore

Passenger service withdrawn	1 January 1952	Stations closed	Date
Distance	12½ miles	Bellurgan	1 January 1952
Company	Dundalk, Newry & Greenore Railway	Annaloughan Halt	1 January 1952
		Gyles Quay Halt	1 January 1952
Stations closed	Date	Bush	1 January 1952
Dundalk Quay Street	1 January 1952	Crossalaney Halt	1 January 1952
Bellurgan Point Halt	1 January 1952	Greenore	1 January 1952

Greenore Station, 4 June 1932.

The Dundalk, Newry & Greenore Railway is one of those peculiar lines that Ireland is so well known for. Owned by the English London & North Western Railway and remaining in English ownership until closure, the line was pure LNWR in all appearances. The LNWR were keen to divert the lucrative cattle traffic away from Dublin to Greenore, a deep water port they were backing. A rail connection to the port was necessary and two companies were formed to provide this, the Dundalk & Greenore Railway and the Newry & Greenore Railway. Although both companies received an Act in 1863, it wasn't until 1869 that construction started on the railway and harbour after the LNWR had provided most of the financial resources. However, the Newry & Greenore were still experiencing difficulties in raising capital and the powers were vested in a renamed company, the Dundalk, Newry & Greenore Railway, in 1873.

The interior of Greenore Station in 1949 with a typical LNWR carriage to the right.

The line was opened from Windmill Road Junction in Dundalk to Greenore on 1 May 1873. Only three stations were provided upon opening, the DNGR Dundalk Quay Street Station, Bellurgan and Greenore. The DNGR had running powers from the Dublin & Belfast Junction Railway station and trains started from there, involving a reversal out to Dundalk West Junction on the Dundalk & Enniskillen line, then eastwards across the square crossing, where the line crossed the Dublin—Belfast line at right angles on the flat, through Barrack Street Station before reaching Windmill Road Junction. Windmill Road Junction was an end-on junction and it was at this point that the DNGR trains reached their own metals before arriving at their own Dundalk station, Quay Street. From there the trains would run along the coast to Greenore. Three large viaducts were built - the 22-span Castletown Viaduct, the 22-span Ballymascanlon Viaduct and the Riverstown Viaduct. The trains consisted of LNWR carriages (in purple-brown and spilt milk livery) hauled by Crewe-built saddle tanks. The ferries ran from Greenore to Holyhead but never achieved the traffic levels predicted or times from Dublin. Partition caused problems for the line as it started in the Free State and ended up in Newry in the province of Ulster. This was further exacerbated with the 1926 General Strike in Britain which saw the cessation of passenger sailings (and passengers had never been overly keen on sharing the boat with cattle and general goods). In 1933 an agreement was reached with the Great Northern Railway of Ireland to run the daily operation of the line, thus saving the LMS sending men to attend to the stock. One innovation of the GNR(I) was to introduce a railbus service in 1935. To coincide with its introduction, four new halts were opened on 7 July at Bellugan Point, Annaloughan, Gyles Quay and Crossalaney. Losses continued to mount and in 1950 the British Transport Commission, the owners since British nationalisation in 1948, decided to close the line to all traffic on 1 January 1952. A small section of line survived between Windmill Road Junction and St George's Quay in Dundalk for a few more years until this too was closed around 1955 by the Republic's Minister for Industry and Commerce.

Dundalk to Clones

Passenger service withdrawn	14 October 1957	*Stations closed*	*Date*
Distance	39½ miles	Culloville	14 October 1957
Company	Great Northern Railway of Ireland	Ballybay	14 October 1957
		Monaghan Road	14 October 1957
Stations closed	*Date*	Newbliss	14 October 1957
Dundalk Barrack Street *	1893	Clones	14 October 1957
Dundalk Clarke **	Open		
Kellybridge Halt	14 October 1957	* No passenger train is known to have used this station.
Inniskeen	14 October 1957	** Originally named Dundalk Junction until 10 April 1966; it remains
Blackstaff Halt	14 October 1957	open on the Dublin—Belfast main line.

Newbliss Station. Note the lamp between the track for illuminating the crossing.

Clones Station, 18 April 1955. On the left is GNR(I) U class No. 197 with the 12.50 p.m. service to Enniskillen and GNR(I), while on the right is Ps class No. 72 with the 12.45 p.m. departure to Cavan.

The line from Dundalk to Clones (and ultimately to Londonderry) was a sprawling line that took a long time to build by a number of different companies. The first attempt got off to a false start with the Dundalk & Western Railway. The D&W received an Act as early as 1837 to build a line to Ballybay, between Castleblayney and Clones. Although the first sod was turned to great ceremony in 1839, the project ended up being abandoned. It was an attempt by a later company, the Dundalk & Enniskillen Railway, that had more success. Receiving an Act in July 1845, the intention was to build a line from Dundalk to Enniskillen. However, the D&E were only going to build as far as Clones. The remaining section from Clones to Enniskillen was to be built by the Newry & Enniskillen Railway, with the D&E sharing the expense and the responsibilities with the N&E. In the event the poorly run N&E did not reach Clones or Enniskillen and the powers to build this section were transferred to the D&E. Construction commenced at the Dundalk end in October 1845, but progress was slow. The first section to Castleblayney was not completed until 1849 when the line opened to traffic on 15 February. Two intermediate stations were provided at Inniskeen and Culloville.

Extension to Clones met with difficulty as the line had to traverse both rocky land and peat bogs. A shortage of money also delayed construction and further Acts were required to extend the powers. Ballybay was the next point reached and the line was opened on 17 July 1854. Construction continued, with the line opening to Newbliss on 14 August 1855 and finally to Clones on 7 July 1858. The building of this line at the Dundalk end led to one of the best known railway features in Ireland, the Square Crossing. As Barrack Street Station was on the eastern side of the town, the line had to cross the Dublin & Belfast Junction Railway. It did so on the level and at right angles just south of the D&BJR station. This crossing was of great concern to the Board of Trade on safety grounds and was the scene of many collisions and other incidents. Further powers were obtained to build a branch from Shantonagh, near Ballybay, to Cavan via Cootehill. In the event the Ulster Railway-backed Clones & Cavan Extension Railway put paid to this and the branch ended at Cootehill, opening on 18 October 1860. Meanwhile, the D&E took lease of the Londonderry & Enniskillen Railway and commenced through running over the entire line. In 1862 the D&E changed its name to the Irish North Western Railway. This change was relatively short lived as the Irish North Western found itself in financial difficulty and it must have been a relief to the shareholders when the company merged into the Northern Railway of Ireland on 1 January 1876, this itself becoming the Great Northern Railway of Ireland just four months later on 1 April. In 1859 a new station called Monaghan Road was provided between Ballybay and Newbliss. The monopoly at Clones was short lived, lasting until 7 April 1862 when the Clones & Cavan Extension Railway opened their line to Cavan. The following year the Ulster Railway arrived at Clones from Portadown on 2 March. Another branch line, from Inniskeen to Carrickmacross, was opened on 31 July 1886. The next problem occurred with the formation of the Irish Free State in the south and the Province of Ulster in 1921. Partition ensued and the GNR(I), running railways in both states, was left as an independent operator. On the Irish North, the town of Culloville found itself in Ulster, whereas the station, being on the other side of the river and south of the border, was in the Free State.

In 1924 a new stop was provided at Kellysbridge Halt, between Dundalk and Inniskeen. A further halt was opened in 1927 at Blackstaff, between Inniskeen and Culloville. Post-war Ireland saw a growth in road transport which affected the fortunes of the GNR(I). In an effort to fight back, the GNR(I) introduced a railcar service on the Irish North in 1935. With the ability to stop almost anywhere, a number of additional stops were provided, mainly at level crossings. A total of thirteen railcar stops were provided and were in use until the 1940s. Although the Second World War increased traffic on the railways, this was to be short lived. After the war the GNR(I) found itself in financial difficulty, announcing it would cease running services in Ulster in 1951. The announcement caused the governments of the Republic and Province to act and they jointly purchased the company, which became the Great Northern Railway Board in 1953.

A difference in view over provision of rail services proved to be the end of the line when the Northern government proposed the closure of some 115 miles of GNRB track, including the Newtownbutler to Omagh section of the Irish North. Despite an enquiry, the Northern government insisted upon the closures with services ceasing at the end of September 1957. This led to an odd situation with a major section of the Dundalk—Londonderry line gone. The Republic's government had little choice but to apply for closure of the remaining parts and branches of the line. However, legislation could not be introduced so quickly and this led to the Dundalk—Clones stump being operated for a further couple of weeks before being closed to passengers on 14 October 1957. Meanwhile, the Northern government had announced its intention in June 1957 to end the 1953 agreement to jointly operate the GNRB. As a result, the GNRB ceased to exist from October 1958. All the former GNRB lines in the Republic were passed to Córas Iompair Éireann. Although passenger services had ceased on the Dundalk—Clones section, goods services continued to run until these were discontinued and the line closed completely on 1 January 1960. The goods yard at Barrack Street in Dundalk continued to be used by CIÉ with access from the south junction until 1995.

Inniskeen to Carrickmacross

Passenger service withdrawn	10 March 1947
Distance	$6\frac{1}{2}$ miles
Company	Great Northern Railway of Ireland

Stations closed	*Date*
Inniskeen *	10 March 1947
Essexford	1925
Carrickmacross	10 March 1947

* Closed as a junction but remained open on the main line until 14 October 1957.

GNR(I) QGs class No. 153 runs around at Carrickmacross Station.

With the merger of the Irish North Western Railway into the Northern Railway and subsequently the Great Northern Railway of Ireland, a period of consolidation took place in the new empire before further expansion. Ever on the lookout for other profitable routes, a branch was proposed to the town of Carrickmacross in 1881. Land purchase delayed construction of the branch for nearly two years, but it finally opened for traffic on 31 July 1886. The six and a half mile branch left the Irish North at Inniskeen and ran south-west to Essexford, which received a station a little later in 1887, before turning east to Carrickmacross. The branch had a fairly uneventful life until Essexford Station was closed in 1922. The station was reopened again in 1925. 1947 saw the GNR(I) suspend passenger services on 10 March due to the fuel shortage caused by the miners' strike in Britain and a hard winter. In the event, the branch was never reopened to passengers. Goods services continued and the line passed to the GNRB in 1953 before being finally acquired by CIÉ in 1958 upon the dissolution of the GNRB. As has been recounted in the previous chapter, CIÉ were left with a stump of the former Irish North and, along with the remains of the main line, the branch closed completely on 1 January 1960.

Ballybay to Cootehill

Passenger service withdrawn	10 March 1947
Distance	9 miles
Company	Great Northern Railway of Ireland

Stations closed	*Date*
Ballybay *	10 March 1947
Rockcorry	10 March 1947
Cootehill	10 March 1947

* Remained open on the main line until 14 October 1957.

The station staff at Cootehill.

GNR(I) QGs class No. 154, built by the North British Locomotive Company in 1904, standing at Cootehill with two six-wheeler carriages.

The other branch off the Irish North ran from Shantonagh Junction near Ballybay to Cootehill. The branch was originally intended by the Dundalk & Enniskillen Railway to reach Cavan, but with the Ulster Railway rapidly reaching Clones and heavily backing the Clones & Cavan Extension Railway it became clear to the D&E that the UR would get there first. As a result, the D&E terminated the branch at Cootehill and abandoned the Cavan section. The branch opened for traffic on 18 October 1860 with one intermediate station at Rockcorry. In 1876 the D&E merged into the Northern Railway, which itself became the Great Northern Railway of Ireland later in the same year.

The hard winter of 1947 combined with a British miners' strike led to fuel shortages in Ireland and as a result the GNR(I) suspended passenger services on the branch on 10 March 1947. Although the fuel situation eased later, the branch was not reopened to passengers. Goods trains, mainly consisting of cattle specials, continued to run as control of the branch passed to the Great Northern Railway Board in 1953, but the end finally came when the GNRB closed the branch completely on 20 June 1955. Ballybay Station on the main line remained open for a few more years until passenger services were withdrawn from the Irish North in 1957.

Glaslough to Clones

Passenger service withdrawn	14 October 1957
Distance	$17\frac{1}{2}$ miles
Company	Great Northern Railway of Ireland

Stations closed	*Date*
Glaslough	14 October 1957
Monaghan (old station)	1863
Monaghan (new station)	14 October 1957
Smithborough	14 October 1957
Clones	14 October 1957

The imposing exterior of Monaghan Station.

The Ulster Railway opened its line from Belfast to Portadown in 1842. Having reached Portadown, the UR required a new Act in 1845 to continue on to Armagh. Armagh was reached three years later with the line opening on 1 March 1848. Beyond Armagh there were numerous small towns engaged in the linen industry so further Acts were obtained in 1855 to extend to Monaghan and in 1856 to reach Clones. The line to Monaghan opened for traffic on 25 May 1858 and intermediate stations were provided at Killylea, Tynan and Glaslough.

GNR(I) Ps class 4-4-0 No. 72, built by Beyer, Peacock, standing ready at Clones with the 12.45 p.m. service to Cavan, 18 April 1955.

When construction on the extension from Monaghan to Clones was started, it diverged from the existing line just north of Monaghan Station. When completed, the extension opened for traffic on 2 March 1863 with a new station at Monaghan being provided (the original Monaghan Station closed the same day). Just one intermediate station was provided at Smithborough. At Clones the Ulster Railway met up with the Dundalk & Enniskillen Railway which had reached the town from Dundalk five years earlier. In 1876 the Ulster Railway merged with the Northern Railway to form the Great Northern Railway of Ireland, leaving all lines converging on Clones under the control of one company. The establishment of the Irish Free State in 1921 and subsequent partition had a marked effect on the line. The natural traffic flow was from Clones to Belfast, but as Clones was in Co. Monaghan, which was in the Free State, this pattern was disrupted. The GNR(I) was forced to make economies and the line was singled from Clones to Monaghan in 1932. Although the fortunes of the GNR(I) were temporarily increased with wartime traffic from 1939, the post-war period saw the company in financial difficulty. By 1951 the situation was bad, with the GNR(I) announcing widespread closures in Ulster that year. The governments of the Republic and the Province came to the rescue jointly working the company under the new name of the Great Northern Railway Board in 1953.

The GNR(I) were early users of diesel railcars. Here, No. 616 - built by the GNR(I) at Dundalk in 1951 from a kit supplied by Park Royal - heads a three-car train at Clones, 18 April 1955.

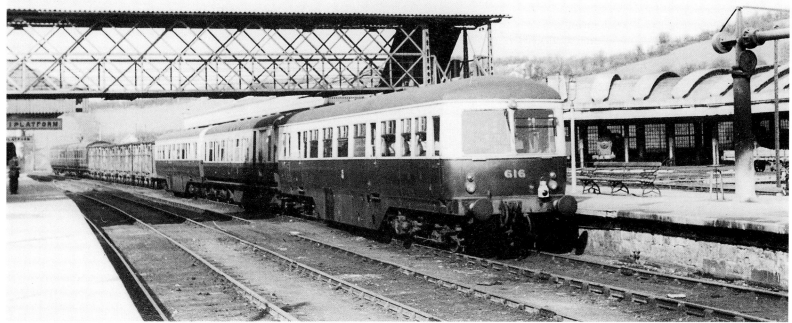

This reprieve proved to be temporary when in 1956 the Northern government announced widespread closures to the system in Ulster, including the Portadown to Tynan section of this line. This proposal would have left the line as an unworkable stump from Clones to Glaslough. Despite enquiries and tribunals, the Northern government eventually had its way and gave notice to the Board in June 1957 that services were to cease by the end of September. The services did cease and the Portadown to Glaslough section was closed on 1 October 1957. This left the GNRB with an unworkable line and they subsequently applied for closure of the Clones to Glaslough section. Time constraints to get the necessary legislation through meant that this stump had to operate for another two weeks before it was closed to passengers on 14 October 1957. The following year saw the GNRB close the Monaghan to Glaslough section completely on 2 February. Along with the original closure notices, the Northern government also announced that they were to end the 1953 agreement for jointly working the GNRB. Subsequent legislation was passed in both Parliaments and the GNRB ceased to exist from 1 October 1958. The company's assets were split between the two states' railway operators with the Clones to Monaghan section passing to Córas Iompair Éireann. The remainder of the line did not last long; CIÉ closed the remaining section on 1 January 1960.

Clones to Cavan

Passenger service withdrawn	14 October 1957
Distance	$15\frac{1}{2}$ miles
Company	Great Northern Railway of Ireland

Stations closed	*Date*
Clones	14 October 1957
Redhills	14 October 1957
Ballyhaise *	14 October 1957
Loreto College Halt	14 October 1957
Cavan	14 October 1957

* Formerly Belturbet Junction; renamed in 1885.

Redhills Station, 18 April 1955.

JT class 2-4-2T No. 95, built in 1898, standing at the platform with the 4.40 p.m. from Belturbet at Ballyhaise Station, 17 May 1950.

The Ulster Railway had extended its Belfast—Portadown line through to Armagh and Monaghan in 1858. From Monaghan, the UR intended to continue to Clones and Cavan. An Act of 1856 authorised the extension to Clones which was reached in 1863. Meanwhile, the Dublin & Enniskillen Railway had reached Clones in 1858 and also had plans to reach Cavan. The D&E intended to do this via Cootehill with a branch from Shantonagh Junction near Ballybay. As there were several interested parties involved, a separate company, the Clones & Cavan Extension Railway, was set up and received an Act on 1 August 1859. The Act allowed financial contributions from the Ulster, Dublin & Drogheda, Dublin & Belfast Junction and Dublin & Enniskillen Railways, with the latter company building and operating the line. Construction was completed and the line was opened for traffic on 7 April 1862. One intermediate station, Belturbet Junction, was provided. At the time of opening the branch to Belturbet had not been built and would not be completed until 1885, whereupon the station would change its name to Ballyhaise.

Ballyhaise Station, looking towards Cavan, 18 May 1955.

On leaving Clones, the Cavan line ran parallel to the Enniskillen line for three-quarters of a mile before turning south. At Cavan, the Clones & Cavan Extension Railway used the Midland Great Western Railway station, which the latter company had opened in 1856. Redhills, between Clones and Belturbet Junction, received a station in 1872. The line came under control of the Great Northern Railway of Ireland in 1876 with the formation of that company. One change with the new ownership was that the service pattern altered so that trains ran from Cavan through to Belfast.

Loreto College Halt, 18 April 1955. This was opened in 1930 to serve a local college.

1921 saw the establishment of the Irish Free State and the Province of Ulster. In 1924, railways operating entirely in the Free State were amalgamated to form the Great Southern Railways. As the GNR(I) operated lines in both states, it was left as an independent operator. One effect of this political change was partition and although Clones and Cavan were both in the south, the line crossed the political border no less than six times between Clones and Redhills. However, as this part of the country was sparsely inhabited it was treated as being in the south and avoided the Customs checks carried out at other border crossings. In 1930 a new station, Loreto College Halt, opened two miles north of Cavan to serve a local school.

GNR(I) Ps class 4-4-0 No. 105, standing ready to leave Cavan with the 11.45 a.m. service to Clones, 18 April 1955.

The post-war financial crisis of the GNR(I) led to the governments of the Republic and the Province jointly purchasing and working the company, which became the Great Northern Railway Board in 1953. This solution proved temporary when in 1956 the Northern government announced proposals to close some 115 miles of railway in Ulster, including the Portadown to Tynan section of the route, removing the through route from Cavan to Belfast. Despite enquiries and tribunals, the Northern government had its way and the Board was informed that services would cease at the end of September 1957.

With the through route gone, the GNRB applied for permission to close the remaining parts of the affected system. Although permission was given, it took a further two weeks to get the legislation through before passenger services were discontinued on the Clones—Cavan line, which closed on 14 October 1957. Meanwhile, the Northern government had announced in June 1957 that it intended ending the 1953 agreement to jointly operate the GNRB. Legislation was put through both parliaments to end the GNRB and on 1 October 1958 it ceased to exist. The property and assets were split between the Ulster Transport Authority and Córas Iompair Éireann, with the Cavan line passing to CIÉ. It took just over a year before CIÉ closed the line completely on 1 January 1960.

Ballyhaise to Belturbet

Passenger service withdrawn	14 October 1957
Distance	$4\frac{1}{4}$ miles
Company	Great Northern Railway of Ireland

Stations closed	*Date*
Ballyhaise *	14 October 1957
Belturbet **	14 October 1957

* Formerly Belturbet Junction.

** Cavan & Leitrim trains used a bay platform until 1 April 1959.

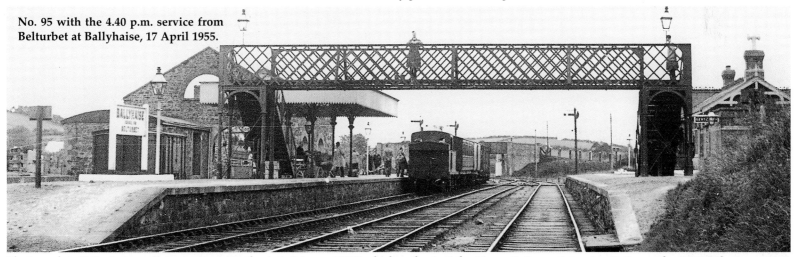

No. 95 with the 4.40 p.m. service from Belturbet at Ballyhaise, 17 April 1955.

The branch to Belturbet was first mentioned in the Act of August 1859 which authorised the Clones & Cavan Extension Railway. The C&CER had a number of supporters including the Dublin & Drogheda, Dublin & Belfast Junction, Ulster and Dublin & Enniskillen Railways. Although the UR were the largest supporters, it was left to the D&E to build and operate the lines. Although the Cavan line opened for traffic on 7 April 1862 with an intermediate station called Belturbet Junction, it was some time later before the branch was built. The finances of the D&E were not good and in July 1862 an Act was passed which not only allowed the company to change its name to the Irish North Western Railway, but also allowed it to raise some £300,000 to complete the Belturbet line and other unfinished work. Despite this, the fortunes of the Irish North worsened and the branch was not completed. On 1 January 1876 the Irish North merged into the Northern Railway, which itself was short lived as the Ulster Railway merged with it to form the Great Northern Railway of Ireland in April of the same year. A period of consolidation was entered into before the GNR(I) started to plan other profitable branches. The Belturbet branch was once again considered and a new Act in 1881 was required to revive the powers to build the line. However, land purchase was slow and delayed the start of construction for over two years. The line was completed and opened for traffic on 26 June 1885. The original junction station on the Cavan line was called Belturbet Junction in anticipation of the branch. However, upon the opening of the branch, the station changed its name to Ballyhaise.

No. 95, ready to leave with a train to Ballyhaise, 17 April 1955. Belturbet was a mixed gauge station with the 3 feet gauge Cavan & Leitrim line using the other end of the station.

By October 1887, the Cavan & Leitrim narrow gauge railway had reached Belturbet and the station became a mixed gauge station. There was a steady flow of cattle and coal traffic from the C&L which was transhipped to the GNR(I) for onward travel. The coal traffic remained manually handled right up until closure. The formation of the Irish Free State in 1921 and subsequent partition meant that the branch found itself in a different state to the rest of the GNR(I) system. In 1924 the new government of the Free State amalgamated the railways running wholly within the Free State into the Great Southern Railways while companies operating in both states were left independent. As such, the C&L became the Cavan & Leitrim Section of the GSR whereas the GNR(I) remained independent. After the Second World War the hard winter and British miners' strike of 1947 caused fuel shortages. Passenger traffic on the C&L was suspended from 24 February 1947 with the broad gauge services following on 10 March. When the situation eased, services were restored on the C&L on 24 May with the broad gauge following on 2 June. The GNR(I)'s financial crisis in the 1950s resulted in the formation of the Great Northern Railway Board in 1953 when the two governments jointly purchased and operated the railway. In the event, this was a short-lived reprieve for the GN as in 1956 the Northern government announced proposals to close a number of lines in Ulster, including the Portadown to Tynan section of the Clones—Belfast route, which would disrupt the traffic flows. Despite protestations and enquiries, the Northern government persisted and announced that the closures would take place at the end of September 1957. With part of the system closed, the GNRB applied for permission to close the remaining parts of the affected system. Although permission was given, it took a further two weeks for necessary legislation to pass through Parliament. The Ballyhaise to Belturbet branch closed to passengers on 14 October 1957. Meanwhile, the Northern government had also announced that it would be ending the 1953 agreement to jointly work the line. With the necessary legislation put through the two Parliaments, the GNRB ceased to exist on 1 October 1958. The assets of the GNRB were split between the UTA and CIÉ. The Clones—Cavan and Belturbet branch were passed to CIÉ. With the closure of the Cavan & Leitrim section on 1 April 1959, the branch's freight traffic had gone and it too closed on the same day.

Inny Junction to Cavan

Passenger service withdrawn	27 January 1947	*Stations closed*	*Date*
Distance	24¼ miles	Drumhowna	27 January 1947
Company	Midland Great Western Railway	Crossdoney	27 January 1947
		Cavan **	27 January 1947
Stations closed	*Date*		
Inny Junction *	1931	* Formerly Cavan Junction; renamed in 1878.	
Float	27 January 1947	** Closed to CIÉ passengers on 27 January 1947; closed to GNRB passengers on 14	
Ballywillan	27 January 1947	October 1957.	

Cavan had long featured in various promotions for rail connection. The first proposal came as early as 1836 by the Great Central Irish Railway and subsequently by various other schemes. After considerable debate and negotiation with other companies, the Midland Great Western Railway announced their intention to extend from Mullingar to Cavan and Longford in 1851. The Cavan branch left the Mullingar—Longford line just under eleven miles from Mullingar in a remote spot of country. The junction was known, predictably enough, as Cavan Junction with the line then running north with stations provided at Float, Ballywillan, Crossdoney and Cavan. The line was opened for traffic on 8 July 1856, but traffic was disappointing with some trains running empty. The MGWR were not deterred as they saw the branch as part of a larger scheme to tap into traffic further north and surveyed a route to Clones with an application being received by Parliament in 1858. In the event, the extension was never built and it was left up to the Clones & Cavan Extension Railway, backed by a consortium of companies, to build the line. It opened in 1862.
Cavan Station had an unusual arrangement once the Clones & Cavan Extension Railway reached the town. The new railway had running powers into the Midland station and the platform was divided in half, separated by a short passenger bridge at platform level. The MGWR used the southern section while the other company used the north. There was a through road to provide a connection between the two companies.
In 1876 an additional station was opened at Drumhowna, between Ballywillan and Crossdoney, and in 1878 Cavan Junction was renamed Inny Junction. A branch line from Crossdoney to Killeshandra was opened in 1886 and is listed in the next section.
The MGWR became part of the Great Southern Railway in 1924. The GSR, forced to make operational economies, closed Inny Junction to passengers in 1931 with passengers changing at Multyfarnham. The signal cabin was also closed and the junction became remotely operated with power points.
The Cavan branch did not escape the wartime fuel shortage and passenger services were suspended from 24 April 1944. When passenger services were resumed on 10 December 1945 it was by then under the control of Córas Iompair Éireann. The hard winter and the British miners' strike of 1947 once again caused services to be suspended. The passenger service was suspended on 27 January with the goods service following on 10 March. Passenger services were never resumed, but the goods service was restored on 3 June, continuing until 1 January 1960 when the branch was closed completely.

Crossdoney to Killeshandra

Passenger service withdrawn	27 January 1947	*Stations closed*	*Date*
Distance	7 miles	Crossdoney	27 January 1947
Company	Midland Great Western Railway	Arva Road	27 January 1947
		Killeshandra	27 January 1947

In 1880 a request from the townspeople of Killeshandra to the Midland Great Western Railway to build a branch to the town was met favourably and a bill subsequently lodged in Parliament. Work commenced on the branch in 1883, but soon ran into trouble. With a combination of boggy ground, a striking workforce and objections to some of the bridges, the line was not completed for inspection until May 1886. The branch passed the inspection and opened for traffic on 1 June 1886.
The junction for the branch was at Crossdoney on the Inny Junction to Cavan line. The junction faced Cavan and trains usually ran from Killeshandra through to Cavan. One intermediate station was provided on the seven-mile branch at Arva Road, serving the village of the same name some two miles distant. Over the years, a number of northward extensions were proposed, one of them to connect with the Sligo, Leitrim & Northern Counties Railway, but nothing came of them.
The MGWR became part of the Great Southern Railway in 1924 and business continued as before. However, the branch did not escape the wartime fuel shortage and all services were suspended from 24 April 1944. When passenger services were resumed on 10 December 1945 it had a new owner in the form of Córas Iompair Éireann. Passenger services were again suspended on 24 February 1947 due to more fuel shortages caused by the hard winter and the British miners' strike. In the event, the line was never reopened, but it wasn't until 1 March 1955 that the branch was officially closed. The branch was finally lifted between April and August of 1957.

Closed stations on passenger lines still open to passenger services
Howth Junction to Dundalk

Station Closed	Date	Station Closed	Date
Baldoyle	30 July 1846	Dunleer	26 November 1984
Baldungan	1 April 1847	Dromin Junction	1955
Skerries Golf Club Halt	18 September 1967	Castlebellingham	6 September 1976
Ardgillan *	Unknown	Mount Pleasant	1887
Bettystown	October 1847		
Newfoundwell	5 April 1855	* Private station for the Taylor Family.	

Dromin Junction Station, looking towards Belfast, 5 June 1964.

Hill of Down to Athlone

Station Closed	Date	Station Closed	Date
Hill of Down	15 June 1963	Streamstown	15 June 1963
Killucan	15 June 1963	Moate	9 May 1987
Newbrook Racecourse *	1929		
Castletown	15 June 1963	* For race traffic only.	

CIÉ 101 class 0-6-0 No. 186, with a special, and Metropolitan-Vickers A class No. A60 at Hill of Down Station, 14 September 1968.

The gates are closed at Castletown Station, 14 September 1968. In the background is Castletown Station Cabin and just to the left is the token exchange mechanism.

CASTLETOWN STATION CABIN